The Let's Talk Library™

Let's Talk About Living With Your Single Dad

Melanie Ann Apel

The Rosen Publishing Group's
PowerKids Press™
New York

To Kelly Dimopoulos Lentine (and Tom, Henry, and Fay). Who'd have thought? Love, Melanie

Published in 2001 by The Rosen Publishing Group, Inc.
29 East 21st Street, New York, NY 10010

First Edition

Book Design: Maria Melendez

Photo Illustrations by Thaddeus Harden

Apel, Melanie Ann.
     Let's talk about living with your single dad / by Melanie Ann Apel
          p. cm.— (The let's talk library)
     Summary: Discusses, in simple text, the difficulties, adjustments, and positive aspects of living with a single male parent.
     ISBN 0-8239-5619-9 (library binding)
     1. Children of single parents—Juvenile literature. 2. Single fathers—Juvenile literature. 3. Father and child—Juvenile literature. [1. Single-parent families. 2. Father and child.] I. Title. II Series.

     HQ777.4 .A64 2000
     306.874'2-dc21   99-088251

Manufactured in the United States of America

Table of Contents

Valerie's Dad

Valerie's dad is very busy. He cooks breakfast. Then he gets Valerie and her brother David ready for school. Valerie's dad is the only parent in their house. He takes care of Valerie and David. He is also in charge of running the house. He even feeds and walks their dog Max. Every day Valerie's dad goes to work in the city. He loves taking care of Valerie and David, but sometimes he gets very tired. It is not always easy being a single dad.

◀ *Single dads have a lot to do every day. This dad is walking his son and daughter to school.*

Love Is What Makes a Family

There are all kinds of families. In some families, mom, dad, and the kids all live in the same house. Some kids live with just one parent. Some kids live with their grandparents. Other kids live with their parents, grandparents, and other relatives. There are kids who live in foster homes. In a foster home, an adult cares for a child who is not a relative. The most important thing about a family is that everyone loves each other very much.

This girl likes to read with her aunt. The most important thing about a family is the love that everyone shares. ▶

Annie's Dad Got a Divorce

Annie's mom and dad didn't get along well. They used to fight all the time. They decided to get a **divorce**. Annie's dad has **custody** of Annie. This means she lives with him. He takes care of Annie. He makes sure she has everything she needs. Annie's mom lives nearby. She sees Annie often. Annie wishes her parents still lived together, but she understands that they are happier apart. She hated to see them fight.

◀ *Divorce is never easy on a family. Even if you live with your dad, though, you can still spend time with your mom.*

When a Mom Dies

Chris lives with his sister Tamara and his dad. Chris's mom died a couple of years ago. A man whose wife has died is called a **widower.** Chris's dad is a widower. He does the best he can to take care of his kids by himself. Sometimes Chris's grandparents come over to watch him and his sister. Chris likes when his grandparents visit. He loves to see them. He also knows that once in a while his dad needs to rest. This doesn't mean Chris's dad loves him or Tamara any less. He just might need some quiet time alone.

Grandparents can be a comfort to your dad if he is a widower. They are also a lot of fun to have around! ▶

Single Dads Work Hard

Single dads are **responsible** for their kids. It is their job to take care of their children. Single dads have to do the work of two parents. They cook and clean. They help with homework and coach Little League. If your dad is a single dad, he has a lot to do every day. Let him know that you **appreciate** how hard he works. Your dad will feel happy knowing that he is doing a good job.

◀ When your dad helps you with your homework, let him know how much it means to you.

Dad on a Date

Your dad loves spending time with you. He also likes to spend time with other grown-ups. Sometimes he might go out with a group of friends from work. Maybe he goes on dates with women. They might go out to dinner or to a movie. Sometimes they might just sit and talk. It is important for your dad to go out with other grown-ups, just like you need to play with other kids.

Your dad needs to spend time with other grown-ups. Help him get ready to go out. It will give you extra time together. ▶

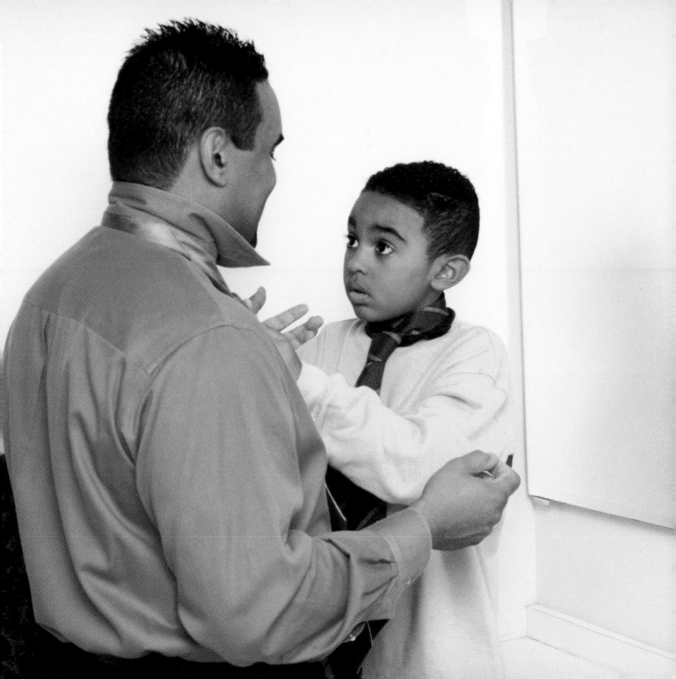

Dad's New Wife

Does your dad spend a lot of time with one special woman? Maybe he calls her his girlfriend. She makes him feel loved and special. Your dad might decide to marry the new woman in his life. It is okay for you to be upset about this. It is also okay for you to like this woman. That doesn't mean she is going to take the place of your mother. Talk to your dad about what you are feeling. He may have a new wife, but he still loves you very much. He wants to do all he can to make you feel safe and happy.

◀ *Talk to your dad about the woman in his life. He loves you and wants to know what you are feeling.*

Someone to Listen

There will be days when your dad is so busy he can't sit and talk with you. Sometimes you may not even want to talk to your dad about certain things. If your mom is not around, try talking to a grandparent or an aunt. You might have a teacher or coach you feel close to. You can also speak to **guidance counselors** at school. Guidance counselors are happy to listen to any problems you might have. They might be able to offer some helpful advice.

A guidance counselor is a great person to talk to. They care about your problems and can offer advice. ▶

Helping Out

Single dads have tough jobs. They love you very much, but it is not easy to get everything done. You can help your dad. Learn to run the dishwasher. Make your bed by yourself. Let your dad sleep late on the weekends. Ask your dad for ways you can help. Respect his rules. He sets these rules for your safety. Most of all let your dad know that he is doing a great job and that you love him.

Help your dad around the house. This girl is doing a great job of making her bed! Her help means a lot to her dad.

On the Same Team

You and your dad have a special relationship. You have fun together. You work through your problems. You help each other out. Life is not always easy. Things happen that we don't expect. Your dad loves you though, and is always on your side. He will be there to give you comfort and advice. The closeness you have with your dad will never go away. That's what makes you such a terrific team!

Glossary

appreciate (uh-PREE-shee-ayt) To be thankful for something or someone.

custody (KUS-tuh-dee) Direct responsibility for care and control of kids.

divorce (dih-VORS) The legal ending of a marriage.

guidance counselors (GY-dins KOWN-suh-lerz) People who help students solve personal problems or problems with other people.

widower (WIH-doh-er) A man whose wife has died.

responsible (rih-SPON-sih-bul) Being the one to take care of someone or something.

Index